This journal belongs to

..................................................................................................

Date

..................................................................................................

Start where you are. Use what you have. Do what you can.

ARTHUR ASHE

In the long run, the sharpest weapon of all is a kind and gentle spirit.

ANNE FRANK

.................................................................................................................................

.................................................................................................................................

.................................................................................................................................

.................................................................................................................................

.................................................................................................................................

.................................................................................................................................

.................................................................................................................................

.................................................................................................................................

.................................................................................................................................

.................................................................................................................................

.................................................................................................................................

.................................................................................................................................

.................................................................................................................................

.................................................................................................................................

.................................................................................................................................

.................................................................................................................................

.................................................................................................................................

.................................................................................................................................

.................................................................................................................................

.................................................................................................................................

.................................................................................................................................

.................................................................................................................................

.................................................................................................................................

May our lives be illumined by the steady radiance renewed daily,
of a wonder, the source of which is beyond reason.

DAG HAMMARSKJÖLD

The true sign of intelligence is not knowledge but imagination.

ALBERT EINSTEIN

Blessed are those who find wisdom, those who gain understanding.

THE BIBLE

The highest form of wisdom is kindness.

THE TALMUD

I feel gratitude in my heart each time
I can meet someone and look at his or her smile.

ELIE WIESEL

True silence is the rest of the mind, and is to the spirit
what sleep is to the body, nourishment and refreshment.

WILLIAM PENN

The tree that is beside the running water is fresher and gives more fruit.

TERESA OF AVILA

I can't change the direction of the wind,
but I can adjust my sails to always reach my destination.

JIMMY DEAN

Everybody is unique. Compare not yourself with anybody else
lest you spoil God's curriculum.

BAAL-SHEM-TOV

Accept the challenges so that you can feel the exhilaration of victory.

GEORGE S. PATTON

People will forget what you said...
but people will never forget how you made them feel.

MAYA ANGELOU

A random act of kindness, no matter how small,
can make a tremendous impact on someone else's life.

ROY T. BENNETT

Life is 10 percent what happens to you and 90 percent how you react to it.

CHARLES R. SWINDOLL

Love is when the other person's happiness is more important than your own.

H. JACKSON BROWN JR.

We are closer to God when we are asking questions
than when we think we have the answers.

ABRAHAM JOSHUA HESCHEL

A single candle can light a thousand more without diminishing itself.

HILLEL THE ELDER

Above all else, guard your heart, for everything you do flows from it.

THE BIBLE

Perfection is not attainable,
but if we chase perfection we can catch excellence.

VINCE LOMBARDI

He that gives should never remember;
he that receives should never forget.

THE TALMUD

Every great dream begins with a dreamer.

HARRIET TUBMAN

Faith is the strength by which a shattered world shall emerge into the light.

HELEN KELLER

To be kind is more important than to be right.

Laughter is the most beautiful and beneficial therapy
God ever granted humanity.

CHUCK SWINDOLL

Two are better than one....
If either of them falls down, one can help the other up.

THE BIBLE

A little bit of light dispels a lot of darkness.

RABBI SCHNEUR ZALMAN OF LIADI

One question is always relevant: How can I use this to move forward?

REBBETZIN TZIPORAH HELLER

Don't be afraid of discovering that the "real you"
may be different than the "current you."

RABBI NOAH WEINBERG

How wonderful it is that nobody need wait a single moment
before starting to improve the world.

ANNE FRANK

When I cannot feel the faith of assurance,
I live by the fact of God's faithfulness.

MATTHEW HENRY

Rest time is not waste time. It is economy to gather fresh strength.

CHARLES SPURGEON

Don't ask what the world needs.
Ask what makes you come alive, and go do it.

The best preacher is the heart; the best teacher is time;
the best book is the world; the best friend is God.

THE TALMUD

Grace creates liberated laughter. The grace of God...is beautiful,
and it radiates joy and awakens humor.

KARL BARTH

As iron sharpens iron, so one person sharpens another.

THE BIBLE

Sometimes all a person needs is not a brilliant mind that speaks
but a kind heart that listens.

Always remember, you have within you the strength, the patience, and the passion to reach for the stars and change the world.

HARRIET TUBMAN

I'll lift you and you lift me, and we'll both ascend together.

JOHN GREENLEAF WHITTIER

Ellie Claire® Gift & Paper Expressions
Franklin, TN 37067
EllieClaire.com
Ellie Claire is a registered trademark of Worthy Media, Inc.

*Star of David* Journal
© 2018 by Ellie Claire
Published by Ellie Claire, an imprint of Worthy Publishing Group, a division
of Worthy Media, Inc.

ISBN 978-1-63326-200-3

Stock or custom editions of Ellie Claire titles may be purchased in bulk for educational,
business, ministry, fundraising, or sales promotional use. For information, please e-mail
info@EllieClaire.com

Cover by Melissa Reagan
Interior design by Bart Dawson

Printed in China

1 2 3 4 5 6 7 8 9 RRD 23 22 21 20 19 18